Triump
The Devotional

Discovering the Me God has called Me to be

Melissa G. Bolden

Copyright © 2017 Melissa G. Bolden

All rights reserved.

ISBN-13:
978-1974584154

ISBN-10:
1974584151:

I believe in God the revelation Bible

I believe in Jesus Christ the revelation Bible

I am a beloved child of Almighty God.

I am saved to eternal life by the blood of Jesus when God is with me every moment of every day/night and I have chosen as my Lord with whom I dwell.

God is willing and able to help me in every thought, decision, and situation.

My greatest privilege is to enjoy God's presence

God owns everything and provides me with everything I need

I have been given authority in Jesus to heal the sick, cast out demons, preach the word by HS

God provides for my children because I love them, have given my life to them.

God protects

Matth. 15:4

Mk 7:10

10:19

Exod 20:12-16

21:17

Deut 5:16-20

Lev. 20:9

DEDICATION

To the men and women who dared to take the challenge with me and
discovered the beauty of who we are in Him.

ACKNOWLEDGMENTS

Unless otherwise noted, Scripture quotations are taken from THE HOLY BIBLE, NEW INTERNATIONAL VERSION® NIV® Copyright © 1973, 1978, 1984 by International Bible Society® Used by permission. All rights reserved worldwide.

Scripture quotations marked NKJV are taken from The Holy Bible, New King James Version®. Copyright © 1982 by Thomas Nelson, Inc. All rights reserved.

Scripture quotations marked NASB are taken from the New American Standard Bible®, Copyright © 1960, 1962, 1963, 1968, 1971, 1972, 1973,1975, 1977, 1995 by The Lockman Foundation Used by permission. (www.Lockman.org)

Scripture quotations marked AMP are taken from the Amplified® Bible, Copyright © 1954, 1958, 1962, 1964, 1965, 1987 by The Lockman Foundation Used by permission." (www.Lockman.org)

Scripture quotations marked (NLT) are taken from the *Holy Bible*, New Living Translation, copyright ©1996, 2004, 2007, 2013 by Tyndale House Foundation. Used by permission of Tyndale House Publishers, Inc., Carol Stream, Illinois 60188. All rights reserved.

Table of Contents

Melissa G. Bolden

The Challenge

Ten weeks, fifty scriptures, and the Holy Spirit will forever change your perception of who you are. We are embarking on a beautiful journey of realizing who we are in Christ! In the next ten weeks, we are going to discover through God's Word that we, as children of the most High, can do all things through Christ who gives us strength. We are going to gain a greater revelation that we are His masterpiece. We are righteous, blessed, accepted, loved, heirs, seated, powerful, and saved. We are going to allow only God's word to define who we are. We are going to be set Triumphantly Free!

I am thankful that you have decided to journey with me for the next 10 weeks. Get ready for a life-changing adventure! To receive the most of this voyage, I encourage you to do the following:

1. Participate daily. Find a quiet spot in your home equipped with a pen and bible.

2. Before you begin, quiet yourself, perhaps play worship music. Invite the Holy Spirit into the process.

3. Ask God to reveal new things to you in His Word as you read. Ask God to speak to your heart.

4. Meditate daily on the included scripture using the MAP method. Memorize, Actualize, and then Personalize the scripture.

Memorize it – meditate on the scripture, quietly repeating it over and over again throughout your day until you can declare it without reading it.

Actualize it – make the scripture real to you. Ask the Holy Spirit to give you a fresh revelation of its meaning; how can you apply this to your daily life? Then journal what you feel the Holy Spirit is speaking to you.

Personalize it – Rewrite the scripture using personal pronouns such as "me" or "I". For instance: "I am the righteousness of God in Christ Jesus". Remind yourself that the scripture applies to you personally.

5. Ask God to show you any lies you believe that contradict the truth found in the Word. Journal the truths God is speaking to your heart and anything else He speaks to you during this time.

6. Hang in there. We have all believed the lies of the enemy for most of our lives. As you begin to fight for freedom, the enemy will not just lie down and acquiesce. But keep fighting for truth. Because God has promised, "Then you will know the truth, and the truth will set you free. (John 8:32)" The word "know" means to understand, perceive. It implies deep intimacy. So as you become deeply acquainted with God's word, you WILL BE SET FREE! It's a promise.

Friends, get ready to change your world!

WEEK 1 – I CAN DO ALL THINGS
(Philippians 4:13)

She was an unlikely candidate to change the world. Young. Female. Single. The bible does not indicate that there was anything particularly special about this young maiden. She was simply a young girl who awaited her wedding day with her fiancé, Joseph.

When greeted by the angel as "highly favored one, blessed are you among women", I wonder if Mary did her best Robert De Niro imitation: "You talkin' to me?"

Mary saw herself as just an ordinary young girl, but God saw her as extraordinary. Mary dreamed of starting a family with Joseph, but God saw her as the mother of the Savior of the world.

When Mary was confronted with lofty ideas such as "conceiving without knowing a man, birthing a child who will be known as the Son of the Highest, delivering a baby who would be King" she naturally questioned "How?" The Angel's response sealed the deal for Mary: "The Holy Spirit will come upon you and overshadow you. For with God, nothing is impossible." A promise and a declaration was all it took for Mary to believe that from her ordinary, extraordinary could happen. Armed with the promise of the Holy Spirit and a belief in the God of the impossible, Mary knew should could birth the King of the World. She could risk losing her fiancé, she could endure the shame and the condemnation of being an unwed mother, she could withstand the scorning looks of the elders, she could do the impossible.

It was over 60 years later, when Apostle Paul summarized Mary's profound revelation: "I can do all things through him who gives me strength." (Philippians 4:13) Mary and Paul realized that with the Holy Spirit and a promise from God, nothing is impossible for the believer. We can be who God says we are. We can do what He says we can do. We can live righteously, free from guilt and condemnation, forgiving freely, loving unconditionally. We can lay hands on the sick and see them recover, we can cast out demons, we can go into all the world and make disciples. We can be who God says we are.

What lie have you believed that says "I can't"? "I can't break the addiction." "I can't lose the weight." "I can't forgive." "I can't love". "I can't forget the past." "I can't start that new business or ministry." "I can't write that book." "I can't reconcile with my family."

Like ordinary Mary, like ordinary Paul, you have been given a promise and you have the Holy Spirit dwelling within you. Therefore, you can look in the mirror and declare with all confidence and assurance:

"I can break this addiction."

"I can lose the weight."

"I can forgive."

"I can love unconditionally."

"I can be healed from past wounds."

"I can start a new business or begin the ministry God has put on my heart."

"I can write that book, preach that sermon, pray for the sick."

"I can reconcile with my family."

"I am armed with a promise, the indwelling of the Holly Spirit and nothing is impossible for God, therefore, I can do all things through Christ who gives me strength."

Daily Prayer for Week 1:

Father, I ask that from your glorious, unlimited resources you would empower me with inner strength through your Spirit. Christ, make your home in my heart so I may trust in you. Let my roots grow deep into your love and keep me strong. Grant me revelation so that I may comprehend how wide, how long, how high, and how deep your love is for me. May I experience the love of Christ and be made complete with the fullness of life and power that comes only from You. Lord, I give you glory because you are able to accomplish infinitely more than I can even ask, think, or imagine through your mighty power at work within me." Reveal your love to me today Lord. In Jesus' name. Amen (Based on Ephesians 3:14-20)

Daily Meditation for Week 1

Day 1 MEMORIZE: "I know what it is to be in need, and I know what it is to have plenty. I have learned the secret of being content in any and every situation, whether well fed or hungry, whether living in plenty or in want. I can do all this through him who gives me strength." (Philippians 4:12 & 13)

ACTUALIZE IT: _____

_____

_____

_____

_____

_____

_____

_____

_____

_____

_____

_____

PERSONALIZE IT: _____

_____

_____

Daily Declaration:

I can _____through Christ who strengthens me.

WEEK 1 DAY 2 MEMORIZE: "Now I'm turning you over to God, our marvelous God whose gracious Word can make you into what he wants you to be and give you everything you could possibly need in this community of holy friends." (Acts 20:32 The Message)

ACTUALIZE IT: _____

_____

_____

_____

_____

_____

_____

_____

_____

_____

_____

_____

_____

_____

_____

PERSONALIZE IT: _____

_____

_____

<u>Daily Declaration</u>:

I can _____ through Christ who strengthens me.

WEEK 1 DAY 3 MEMORIZE: "All Scripture is God-breathed and is useful for teaching, rebuking, correcting and training in righteousness, so that the servant of God may be thoroughly equipped for every good work." (II Timothy 3:16 & 17)

ACTUALIZE IT: _____

_____

_____

_____

_____

_____

_____

_____

_____

_____

_____

_____

_____

_____

_____

_____

_____

PERSONALIZE IT: _____

_____

_____

Daily Declaration:

I can _____through Christ who strengthens me.

WEEK 1 DAY 4 MEMORIZE: "So is my word that goes out from my mouth: It will not return to me empty, but will accomplish what I desire and achieve the purpose for which I sent it." (Isaiah 55:11)

ACTUALIZE IT: _____

_____

_____

_____

_____

_____

_____

_____

_____

_____

_____

_____

_____

_____

_____

_____

_____

PERSONALIZE IT: _____

_____

_____

<u>**Daily Declaration**</u>:

I can _____ through Christ who strengthens me.

WEEK 1 DAY 5 MEMORIZE: "If you remain in me and my words remain in you, ask whatever you wish, and it will be done for you." (John 15:7)

ACTUALIZE IT: _____

_____

_____

_____

_____

_____

_____

_____

_____

_____

_____

_____

_____

_____

_____

_____

PERSONALIZE IT: _____

_____

_____

DAILY DECLARATION:

I can _____through Christ who strengthens me.

WEEK 2 – I AM THE RIGHTEOUSNESS OF GOD
(II Corinthians 5:21)

David was at his lowest. He had lost everything – his family, his possessions, the respect of his men. The voice of accusation was loudly screaming at him. (I Samuel 30)

Internally, I am sure David wrestled with knowing his actions were partly responsible for the predicament he now faced. David had outwardly aligned himself with the Philistines while secretly raiding their outer posts. I'm sure the enemy used this indiscretion to gain a foothold into David's thoughts. The enemy was quick to inwardly shout, "You are not fit to lead. You are just a shepherd boy. Look at what you have done. You have caused your men to lose everything they hold dear and it's all your fault. Saul was right to try to kill you. He knew your arrogance would lead to destruction. Samuel must have been drunk when he anointed you as king." The voice of the enemy lurks, looking for areas of weakness to accuse and disqualify us.

But there were also external voices accusing David. His men, the very men he had done life with for the last few years, the men he had accepted when the world had rejected them, the men with whom he had fought battles, broken bread, laughed with, cried with, now accused him. "Why did you bring us here? We told you it was not wise to be a double agent. You should have killed Saul when you had the opportunity. This is all your fault. Fix this now or we will stone you."

David stood alone. In the midst of the chaos - the internal and external accusations screaming at him - David found clarity by quieting himself. David drew strength from the Lord his God. (I Samuel 30:6b)

I imagine David reminded himself of God's promises for him. I wonder if he replayed Samuel's visit that faithful day when he anointed him king. But then David did something we should all do when the enemy accuses us. He reminded himself he was righteous in God's eyes. David asked for the *ephod* to be brought to him (I Samuel 30:7). The *ephod* was a priestly garment set apart for those who were holy. During intense accusations, David reminded himself that he was holy. This mistake could not, would not, stop God from fulfilling his promises towards him. David, a man who had made a grave mistake, reminded himself that he was righteous and then boldly entered God's throne room of grace and inquired what he should do next. David did not wallow in his failure. He did not beat himself up. He simply went to the Father and found grace.

This is a lesson for each of us. We may have made some mistakes and the enemy is quick to remind us of our shortcomings. But like David, we clothe ourselves in righteousness, remind ourselves of the promises God has spoken to us and we boldly enter into His throne room where we find grace. We silence the voices of accusation with truth and we declare:

"I am the righteousness of God in Christ Jesus. (II Corinthians 5:21) I am holy in his sight, without blemish, and free from accusation (Colossians 1:22)."

Daily prayer for Week 2:

Dear Father, I thank you that I have been baptized in Christ and into His death. Therefore, I walk in the newness of life. I have been united with Him in the likeness of His death and the likeness of His resurrection. I know my old self was crucified with Him and I am no longer a slave of sin, for I have been freed from sin. I am alive in Christ and as such, sin will not reign in my body. It has no dominion over me. I have been liberated from sin and I am now a child of God. I bear fruits of righteousness and have eternal life in God. (Based on Romans 6)

Daily Meditation for Week 2

DAY 1 MEMORIZE: "God made him who had no sin to be sin for us, so that in Him we might become the righteousness of God." (II Corinthians 5:21)

ACTUALIZE IT: _____

_____

_____

_____

_____

_____

_____

_____

_____

_____

_____

_____

_____

_____

PERSONALIZE IT: _____

_____

_____

Daily Declaration:

God made Jesus who knew no sin to be sin on my behalf, so that I could become the righteousness of God in Christ Jesus. (II Corinthians 5:21)

WEEK 2 DAY 2 MEMORIZE: "For if, by the trespass of the one man, death reigned through that one man, how much more will those who receive God's abundant provision of grace and of the gift of righteousness reign in life through the one man, Jesus Christ!" (Romans 5:17)

ACTUALIZE IT: _____

_____

_____

_____

_____

_____

_____

_____

_____

_____

_____

_____

_____

_____

PERSONALIZE IT: _____

_____

_____

Daily Declaration:

God made Jesus who knew no sin to be sin on my behalf, so that I could become the righteousness of God in Christ Jesus. (II Corinthians 5:21)

WEEK 2 DAY 3 MEMORIZE: "For the grace of God has appeared that offers salvation to all people. It teaches us to say "No" to ungodliness and worldly passions, and to live self-controlled, upright and godly lives in this present age." (Titus 2:11-12)

ACTUALIZE IT: _____

_____

_____

_____

_____

_____

_____

_____

_____

_____

_____

_____

_____

PERSONALIZE IT: _____

_____

_____

Daily Declaration:

God made Jesus who knew no sin to be sin on my behalf, so that I could become the righteousness of God in Christ Jesus. (II Corinthians 5:21)

WEEK 2 DAY 4 MEMORIZE: "He himself bore our sins in his body on the cross, so that we might die to sins and live for righteousness; 'by his wounds you have been healed.'" (I Peter 2:24)

ACTUALIZE IT: _____

_____

_____

_____

_____

_____

_____

_____

_____

_____

_____

_____

_____

_____

_____

PERSONALIZE IT: _____

_____

_____

Daily Declaration:

God made Jesus who knew no sin to be sin on my behalf, so that I could become the righteousness of God in Christ Jesus. (II Corinthians 5:21)

WEEK 2 DAY 5 MEMORIZE: "For all have sinned and fall short of the glory of God, and all are justified freely by his grace through the redemption that came by Christ Jesus. God presented Christ as a sacrifice of atonement, through the shedding of his blood—to be received by faith." (Romans 3:23-25a)

ACTUALIZE IT: _____

_____

_____

_____

_____

_____

_____

_____

_____

_____

_____

_____

_____

PERSONALIZE IT: _____

_____

_____

Daily Declaration:

God made Jesus who knew no sin to be sin on my behalf, so that I could become the righteousness of God in Christ Jesus. (II Corinthians 5:21)

WEEK 3 – I AM BLESSED WITH EVERY SPIRITUAL BLESSING

(Ephesians 1:3)

On the other end of the phone was my dear friend. I could tell from the first hello that she was in a difficult place. "Can I come over?" she somehow managed to inquire between the sobs.

When she arrived we sat and talked. Well, she talked; I listened. I felt so inept. I had no words of wisdom to offer. No words to comfort. No action steps to suggest. Her situation was far beyond my expertise. So I sat, listening to my friend, but at the same time, listening to the Holy Spirit. And when she had finished, the Holy Spirit began to speak through me. He gave me words of wisdom, words of comfort, words of healing. He supplied all I needed in that moment.

Paul, wrongfully imprisoned, sat in his jail cell amidst the stench, the darkness, the dire conditions, and wrote, "My God shall supply all your needs according to His riches in glory by Christ Jesus." (Philippians 4:19 NKJV) Such a declaration of faith. Such a trust - not in his own abilities, or the situations that surrounded him - but a simple trust in the faithfulness of God. Paul understood what I was to learn that faith-filled night: "I am blessed with every spiritual blessing."

We are met daily with so many needs – our personal needs, the needs of others - but with every need, we must remember that God has provided abundantly, not according to our abilities, our resources, or our wisdom, but according to His riches.

In the midst of chaos, he provides peace; in the midst of confusion, he provides wisdom; when there is lack, he provides resources. Every need is found in Him. We have been blessed with every spiritual blessing.

Today, lay hold of that promise. You have been given every spiritual gift necessary to eradicate the works of the enemy, advance the Kingdom of God, and impact your world. Despite what you may see with your natural eyes, smell with your natural nose, or hear with your natural ears, stand confident like Paul and declare: "My God shall supply all of my needs according to His riches in glory by Christ Jesus. I have everything I need to face this day."

Daily Prayer for Week 3:

Lord, fill me with the knowledge of your will in all wisdom and spiritual understanding, so that I may walk worthy of you, fully pleasing you, being fruitful in every good work and increasing in the knowledge of you. Lord strengthen me with all might, according to your glorious power so that I may have all patience and long-suffering with joy. Let me give thanks to you. Father, you have qualified me to partake in the inheritance of saints in the light. Father, you have delivered me out of the power of darkness and transferred me into the kingdom of the Son of love. I have redemption through His blood, the forgiveness of sins. Thank you Lord for blessing me with every spiritual gift today and every day. (Based on Colossians 1:9-12)

Daily Meditation for Week 3

DAY 1 MEMORIZE: "Praise be to the God and Father of our Lord Jesus Christ, who has blessed us in the heavenly realms with every spiritual blessing in Christ. For he chose us in him before the creation of the world to be holy and blameless in his sight." (Ephesians 1:3, 4)

ACTUALIZE IT: _____

_____

_____

_____

_____

_____

_____

_____

_____

_____

_____

_____

PERSONALIZE IT: _____

_____

_____

Daily Declaration:

I am blessed with every spiritual blessing in the heavenly places in Christ. (Ephesians 1:3)

WEEK 3 DAY 2 MEMORIZE: "He who did not spare his own Son, but gave him up for us all—how will he not also, along with him, graciously give us all things?" (Romans 8:32)

ACTUALIZE IT: _____

_____

_____

_____

_____

_____

_____

_____

_____

_____

_____

_____

_____

_____

PERSONALIZE IT: _____

_____

_____

Daily Declaration:

I am blessed with every spiritual blessing in the heavenly places in Christ. (Ephesians 1:3)

WEEK 3 DAY 3 MEMORIZE: "The lions may grow weak and hungry, but those who seek the LORD lack no good thing." (Psalm 34:10)

ACTUALIZE IT: _____

_____

_____

_____

_____

_____

_____

_____

_____

_____

_____

_____

_____

_____

_____

_____

PERSONALIZE IT: _____

_____

_____

Daily Declaration:

I am blessed with every spiritual blessing in the heavenly places in Christ. (Ephesians 1:3)

WEEK 3 DAY 4 MEMORIZE: "His divine power has given us everything we need for a godly life through our knowledge of him who called us by his own glory and goodness. Through these he has given us his very great and precious promises, so that through them you may participate in the divine nature, having escaped the corruption in the world caused by evil desires." (II Peter 1:3-4)

ACTUALIZE IT: _____

_____

_____

_____

_____

_____

_____

_____

_____

_____

_____

_____

_____

PERSONALIZE IT: _____

_____

_____

Daily Declaration:

I am blessed with every spiritual blessing in the heavenly places in Christ. (Ephesians 1:3)

WEEK 3 DAY 5 MEMORIZE: "For in him you have been enriched in every way—with all kinds of speech and with all knowledge—God thus confirming our testimony about Christ among you. Therefore you do not lack any spiritual gift as you eagerly wait for our Lord Jesus Christ to be revealed." (I Corinthians 1:5-7)

ACTUALIZE IT: _____

_____

_____

_____

_____

_____

_____

_____

_____

_____

_____

_____

_____

_____

PERSONALIZE IT: _____

_____

_____

Daily Declaration:

I am blessed with every spiritual blessing in the heavenly places in Christ. (Ephesians 1:3)

WEEK 4 – I AM ACCEPTED AND FAVORED
(Ephesians 1:6)

He was known as a traitor, sinner, thief. He was considered beyond redemption. He was hated, scorned, rejected; exiled from the temple. This had become Matthew's life, his identity; an outsider amongst his own people. Perhaps, the money, the parties, the comradery of his fellow tax collectors, had inoculated him from the pain of being rejected by his people. Their rejection perhaps fueled his resolve to steal from and swindle his own people. So Matthew, the tax collector, sat at his booth day in and day out, taking advantage of his own, working for those who oppressed his people. At night, he eased his conscious with loud parties, fast women, and strong ale. This was Matthew's life. But then, suddenly…

That day, Matthew sat at his tax booth like he had done every day before, earning his wealth by cheating his fellow countrymen. Each of them looked at him with disgust, hatred, unforgiveness. But then this Man walked by. Their eyes met. This Man looked at Matthew like no one had in a very long time. There was not hatred, no disgust in his eyes. This man looked past Matt's occupation, past his lifestyle choices, past his hurt, and saw who Matt was called to be – a disciple, a writer of the Gospel, an evangelist, a healer, a son of the Most High. Jesus looked at Matthew and immediately accepted him, immediately extended an invitation to "Come, follow me."

Perhaps it was this unconditional acceptance that prompted a successful businessman to leave all and follow the one who had unconditionally accepted him. Maybe Jesus' acceptance was all that was needed for this former sinner turned disciple to forsake his life of dishonest gain. It is, after all, the goodness of God that leads us to repentance.

Today, Jesus is beckoning us just as He called Matthew 2000 years previously. He looks at us and sees past our sins, past our hurts, past our past. He sees sons and daughters, disciples, teachers, prophets, evangelist, pastors, apostles, writers, businessmen, engineers, and doctors. His acceptance is unconditional. He accepts us even when our behavior is unacceptable.

Brothers and sisters, you have been accepted in the Beloved. Completely. Unconditionally. Eternally. Allow that acceptance to spur you to shed fear of man. (The God of the Universe accepts you, why do you care what anyone else has to say about you?) Allow his acceptance to free you from a life of searching for acceptance through money, prestige, or sin. Rest in his unconditional, free acceptance.

You are accepted in the Beloved. You are highly favored.

DAILY PRAYER FOR WEEK 4:

Lord, I thank you that I dwell in the shelter of the Most High and I rest in the shadow of the Almighty. Lord, you are my refuge and my fortress. You are my God in whom I trust. Surely you will save me from the fowler's snare and from the deadly pestilence. You will cover me with your feathers, and under your wings I will find help; Your faithfulness will be my shield and my rampart. I will not fear the terror of night, nor the arrow that flies by day, nor the pestilence that stalks in the darkness, nor the plaque that destroys at midday. Lord, you are my refuge and I have made you my dwelling place. No harm will overtake me, no disaster will come near my tent. Thank you Lord, that you command your angels concerning me, to guard me in all my ways. I will not strike my foot against a stone. I will tread on the lion and the cobra; I will trample the serpent. Lord, thank you that you rescue me, you protect me, and you acknowledge my name. When I call you, you will answer me. You will be with me in trouble. You will deliver me and honor me. You will satisfy me with long life and show me your salvation. May your favor rest upon me and establish the works of my hand. (Based on Psalms 91 and 90:17)

Daily Meditation for Week 4

DAY 1 MEMORIZE: "To the praise of the glory of His grace, by which He made us accepted in the Beloved." (Ephesians 1:6 NKJV)

ACTUALIZE: _____

_____

_____

_____

_____

_____

_____

_____

_____

_____

_____

_____

_____

_____

PERSONALIZE IT: _____

_____

_____

Daily Declaration:

I am accepted in the beloved. I am highly favored.

WEEK 4 DAY 2 MEMORIZE: "Surely, LORD, you bless the righteous; you surround them with your favor as with a shield." (Psalms 5:12)

ACTUALIZE IT: _____

_____

_____

_____

_____

_____

_____

_____

_____

_____

_____

_____

_____

_____

_____

_____

_____

PERSONALIZE IT: _____

_____

_____

Daily Declaration:

I am accepted in the beloved. I am highly favored.

WEEK 4 DAY 3 MEMORIZE: "May the favor of the Lord our God rest on us; establish the work of our hands for us— yes, establish the work of our hands." (Psalm 90:17)

ACTUALIZE IT: _____

_____

_____

_____

_____

_____

_____

_____

_____

_____

_____

_____

_____

_____

_____

_____

_____

PERSONALIZE IT: _____

_____

_____

Daily Declaration:

I am accepted in the beloved. I am highly favored.

WEEK 4 DAY 4 MEMORIZE: "For he says, "In the time of my favor I heard you, and in the day of salvation I helped you." I tell you, now is the time of God's favor, now is the day of salvation." (II Corinthians 6:2 NIV)

ACTUALIZE IT: _____

_____

_____

_____

_____

_____

_____

_____

_____

_____

_____

_____

_____

_____

_____

_____

PERSONALIZE IT: _____

_____

_____

Daily Declaration:

I am accepted in the beloved. I am highly favored.

WEEK 4 DAY 5 MEMORIZE: "The LORD your God is in your midst, a Warrior who saves. He will rejoice over you with joy; He will be quiet in His love [making no mention of your past sins], He will rejoice over you with shouts of joy." (Zephaniah 3:17 AMP)

ACTUALIZE IT: _____

_____

_____

_____

_____

_____

_____

_____

_____

_____

_____

_____

_____

_____

PERSONALIZE IT: _____

_____

_____

<u>Daily Declaration</u>:

I am accepted in the beloved. I am highly favored.

WEEK 5 – I AM LOVED
(Ephesians 3:17)

Israel sinned. She was the jewel of heaven, God's own special treasure. He fought for her, He delivered her. He provided extravagantly for her. He was faithful to her. But alas, she chose to walk away, to abandon the love of God and pursue the love of more inferior beings. Her sin was egregious.

God was left with only one choice – separation. Hide his face from the very people he loved, the ones He treasured (Isaiah 59:2). He proclaimed, "I will no longer have mercy on the House of Israel. For you are not my people. You are not my wife and I am not your Husband." (Hosea 1:6, 9, 2:2) But this displeased God (Isaiah 59:15). He loved His children with an everlasting, all-encompassing, unconditional love. So He sent His Son, His only Son, to suffer the atrocities of the cross, to carry the burdens of our sins, to be pierced for our iniquities so that His children could forever be rescued, brought back to Him and would never again (regardless to what they do) be separated from Him. He loved us so much that even when we were lost in a life of sin, He redeemed us and brought us back to Him.

Because of the atoning work of Jesus Christ on the cross, God today declares over you:

"I am alluring you and speaking comfort over you." Hosea 2:14

"I will give you vineyards and turn your valleys of trouble into doors of hope where you will sing as in the days of your youth." Hosea 2:15

"Call me 'My Husband' for I will accept you as my wife forever. I will give you justice, fairness, love, kindness, and faithfulness. I will command the sky to send rain on the earth, and it will produce grain, grapes, and olives." Hosea 2:16-22

"I will give you my Spirit and my message. These will be my gifts to you and your families forever. I, the Lord, have spoken." Isaiah 59:21

"Sing and shout. Make your tents larger. You and your children will take over the land." Isaiah 54:1-3

"Don't be afraid, ashamed or discouraged. I will not disappoint you. Forget how sinful you were, stop feeling ashamed. I have taken you back. With love and tenderness, I embrace you. I will have mercy and love you forever! I, your protector and Lord, make this promise." Isaiah 54:6-8

"I have promised that I will never again get angry and punish you. Every mountain and hill may disappear. But I will always be merciful to you. I will not break my agreement to give you peace." Isaiah 54:9-10.

"I will teach your children and make them successful." Isaiah 54:13

"You will be built on fairness, with no fear of injustice. All of your worries shall be taken far from you." Isaiah 54:14

"I will never send anyone to attack you. And you will make prisoners of those who do attack you. Weapons made to attack you will not be successful; words spoken against you shall be cast down. I, the Lord, promise to bless you with victory." Isaiah 54:15-17

"My child, there is absolutely nothing that can separate you from my love. Not trouble, not hard times, not hatred, not hunger, not homelessness, not bullying threats, not backstabbing, not even the even the worst sin. None of this will ever faze you because I love you. Be absolutely convinced, my child, that nothing living or dead, angelic or demonic, today or tomorrow, high or low, thinkable or unthinkable, can get between you and my love for you!" Romans 8:38, 39

Hear what He is declaring over you today. Receive his love today!

Daily Prayer for Week 5:

Dear Father, may Christ dwell in my heart richly. May I be rooted deeply in your love and found securely in your love. May I have the power to comprehend and grasp your devoted love toward me. May I know the length, depth, and height of your love towards me. May I really come to know the love of Christ, which surpasses knowledge and understanding. May I be filled through all my being with the fullness of you and become a body wholly filled and flooded with God Himself. Lord, you are able to do more than I can ever ask, think, desire, hope, or imagine. To You O' Lord be the glory. (Based on Ephesians 3:14 – 20 AMP)

Daily Meditation for Week 5

Day 1 Memorize: "And I pray that you, being rooted and established in love, may have power, together with all the Lord's holy people, to grasp how wide and long and high and deep is the love of Christ, and to know this love that surpasses knowledge—that you may be filled to the measure of all the fullness of God." (Ephesians 3:17b – 19)

ACTUALIZE IT: _____

_____

_____

_____

_____

_____

_____

_____

_____

_____

_____

_____

_____

_____

PERSONALIZE IT: _____

_____

_____

Daily Declaration:

I am rooted and grounded in God's love. (Ephesians 1:6 & 3:17)

Week 5 Day 2 Memorize: "But you, Lord, are a compassionate and gracious God, slow to anger, abounding in love and faithfulness." (Psalm 86:15)

ACTUALIZE IT: _____

_____

_____

_____

_____

_____

_____

_____

_____

_____

_____

_____

_____

_____

_____

PERSONALIZE IT: _____

_____

_____

Daily Declaration:

I am rooted and grounded in God's love. (Ephesians 1:6 & 3:17)

Week 5 Day 3 Memorize: "But because of his great love for us, God, who is rich in mercy, made us alive with Christ even when we were dead in transgressions—it is by grace you have been saved." (Ephesians 2:4 – 5)

ACTUALIZE IT: _____

_____

_____

_____

_____

_____

_____

_____

_____

_____

_____

_____

_____

_____

_____

_____

_____

PERSONALIZE IT: _____

_____

_____

Daily Declaration:

I am rooted and grounded in God's love. (Ephesians 1:6 & 3:17)

Week 5 Day 4 Memorize: "For I am convinced that neither death nor life, neither angels nor demons, neither the present nor the future, nor any powers, neither height nor depth, nor anything else in all creation, will be able to separate us from the love of God that is in Christ Jesus our Lord." (Romans 8:38 – 39)

ACTUALIZE IT: _____

_____

_____

_____

_____

_____

_____

_____

_____

_____

_____

_____

_____

PERSONALIZE IT: _____

_____

_____

<u>**Daily Declaration**</u>:

I am rooted and grounded in God's love. (Ephesians 1:6 & 3:17)

Week 5 Day 5 Memorize: "Love is patient, love is kind. It does not envy, it does not boast, it is not proud. It does not dishonor others, it is not self-seeking, it is not easily angered, it keeps no record of wrongs. Love does not delight in evil but rejoices with the truth. It always protects, always trusts, always hopes, always perseveres. Love never fails." (I Corinthians 13:4-8a)

ACTUALIZE IT: _____

_____

_____

_____

_____

_____

_____

_____

_____

_____

_____

_____

_____

_____

_____

PERSONALIZE IT: _____

_____

_____

Daily Declaration:

I am rooted and grounded in God's love. (Ephesians 1:6 & 3:17)

WEEK 6 – I AM AN HEIR
(Ephesians 1:11)

The coveted and honored birthright. It was bestowed upon the first born son. The birthright allowed the first born son to receive a double portion of his father's inheritance. The eldest son was considered the priest of the family and inherited the judicial authority of his father. Firstborn sons were respected, exalted and favored in their families and communities.

Jesus, God's only begotten son, is considered the firstborn of all creation and the firstborn from the dead (Colossians 1:15, 18). As such, Jesus was loved, honored, and exalted by the Father. He carries the judicial authority of His Father and is our High Priest. Jesus is firstborn among firstborn. He is exalted above all and is seated at the right hand of the Father in a position of honor and power. He is heir to all the Father has.

Yet Jesus does not stand in that position alone. He invites each of us, as sons and daughters, to co-inherit with him (Romans 8:17). He graciously allows each of us to carry the benefits, the honor, the favor of the firstborn. We are priests, we inherit a double portion of our Father's inheritance, and we have the judicial authority of the Father. In this world, we are like Jesus (I John 4:17b)

Unlike Rueben, our birthright cannot be lost. Nor can we, like Esau, give our birthright away. However, the enemy works hard to deceive us from walking in the fullness of our birthright. He uses shame and condemnation to convince us that we are not worthy, we are not equipped, we are not righteous to walk as priests, to wield the authority of our Father.

The truth is, we are heirs, co-heirs with Christ. We are sons and daughters. We have favor, authority, and power. We are well-quipped to push back the darkness and demonstrate the power and love of God. However, each day, every moment of the day, we must choose if we will believe that we are, in fact, heirs. Will we believe that as Jesus was in this world, so are we? Will we trust that the works Jesus did, we can do greater? Will we walk in our birthright as firstborns, or will we trade our authority for the lies of the enemy?

You are heirs, sisters and brothers. Walk in it!

Daily Prayer for Week 6:

Lord, I thank you that you are my Father. I cry out to you as Abba, Father. I ask you to bless me and keep me. Make your face shine upon me and be gracious to me today. Lift up your countenance upon me and give me peace. You have put your name on me and you will bless me. I am yours and you are mine. Thank you that you answer me when I am in distress. Send me help from the sanctuary and grant me support from Zion. Give me the desires of my heart and make all my plans succeed. I will shout for joy and raise a banner in the name of the Lord for I am victorious. Now, I know Lord that you save me for I am your child. I know you answer me from your holy heaven with the saving power of your right hand. Some trust in chariots and some in horses but I trust in my Father, the Lord my God. (Based on Numbers 6:24 – 27, Psalm 20)

Daily Meditation for Week 6:

Day 1 Memorize: "For you are all sons of God through faith in Christ Jesus. And if you are Christ's, then you are Abraham's seed, and heirs according to the promise." (Galatians 3:26, 29 NKJV)

ACTUALIZE IT: _____

_____

_____

_____

_____

_____

_____

_____

_____

_____

_____

_____

PERSONALIZE IT: _____

_____

_____

Daily Declaration:

Because I am united with Christ, I have received an inheritance from God. As Jesus was in this world, so am I. (Ephesians 1:11, I John 4:17)

Week 6 Day 2 Memorize: "For you did not receive the spirit of bondage again to fear, but you received the Spirit of adoption by whom we cry out, "Abba, Father." The Spirit Himself bears witness with our spirit that we are children of God, and if children, then heirs—heirs of God and joint heirs with Christ, if indeed we suffer with Him, that we may also be glorified together." (Romans 8:15 – 17 NKJV)

ACTUALIZE IT: _____

_____

_____

_____

_____

_____

_____

_____

_____

_____

_____

_____

PERSONALIZE IT: _____

_____

_____

Daily Declaration:

Because I am united with Christ, I have received an inheritance from God. As Jesus was in this world, so am I. (Ephesians 1:11, I John 4:17)

Week 6 Day 3 Memorize: "Most assuredly, I say to you, he who believes in Me, the works that I do he will do also; and greater works than these he will do, because I go to my Father." (John 14:12 NKJV)

ACTUALIZE IT: _____

_____

_____

_____

_____

_____

_____

_____

_____

_____

_____

_____

_____

_____

PERSONALIZE IT: _____

_____

_____

Daily Declaration:

Because I am united with Christ, I have received an inheritance from God. As Jesus was in this world, so am I. (Ephesians 1:11, I John 4:17)

Week 6 Day 4 Memorize: "Because you are his sons, God sent the Spirit of his Son into our hearts, the Spirit who calls out, *"Abba,* Father." So you are no longer a slave, but God's child; and since you are his child, God has made you also an heir." (Galatians 4:6-7)

ACTUALIZE IT: _____

_____

_____

_____

_____

_____

_____

_____

_____

_____

_____

_____

_____

_____

_____

PERSONALIZE IT: _____

_____

_____

Daily Declaration:

Because I am united with Christ, I have received an inheritance from God. As Jesus was in this world, so am I. (Ephesians 1:11, I John 4:17)

Week 6 Day 5 Memorize: "This is how love is made complete among us so that we will have confidence on the day of judgment: In this world we are like Jesus." (I John 4:17)

ACTUALIZE IT: _____

_____

_____

_____

_____

_____

_____

_____

_____

_____

_____

_____

_____

PERSONALIZE IT: _____

_____

_____

Daily Declaration:

Because I am united with Christ, I have received an inheritance from God. As Jesus was in this world, so am I. (Ephesians 1:11, I John 4:17)

WEEK 7 – I AM SEATED IN CHRIST
(Ephesians 2:6)

We were all excited about my daughter's upcoming nuptials. I wanted to give her the wedding of her dreams. But as always with me, I like to save a dollar wherever possible. When the caterer offered a ten percent discount for paying in cash, of course I took advantage of the opportunity. I was uncomfortable carrying that amount of cash on my person so I decided to go to a branch of my bank that was closest to the caterer rather than the branch I frequent.

Since I had never in my life stepped foot into this bank, I was prepared to show my driver's license, be fingerprinted, give DNA, or whatever was necessary to withdraw such a large sum from my account. But the teller merely asked me to swipe my bank card, and then he proceeded to prepare the funds I was requesting. But then I became concerned. Can anyone with my bank card just come and withdraw money from my account? So I asked the teller, "Do you need to see my ID?" "No," he replied, "when you swipe your card, your picture appears on my monitor along with your account information."

The teller's explanation not only put me at ease concerning my bank's security measures, but it also gave me insight into spiritual warfare. When I am praying for someone or silencing the enemy, I envision my face showing up in hell with my account information underneath – daughter, favored, loved, righteous, strong, seated in Jesus in Heavenly places. I imagine the demons in hell saying, "Oh, no! That's Melissa. She looks sweet and gentle, but she is a mighty warrior who has kicked some major demonic butt. She knows whose she is and who she is in Christ, she knows her authority over us, and she has sent many of us fleeing. Abort! Abort!"

We are seated in heavenly realms in Christ Jesus, far above all principality, power, might, and dominion (Ephesians 1:21). The enemy is under our feet and God has given us authority and power to trample on his head. As Christians, it's time we begin to walk in our authority, to bind the works of the enemy and release the will of the Father onto this earth.

There is a song with lyrics, "The waves and the winds still know His name."[1] As I was singing that one day, the Lord spoke to me and said, "It's time that the waves and winds know my children's names as well."

Let us not be timid, my friends. Let us be as bold as lions and begin to walk in the authority granted to us as sons and daughters when our eldest brother went to cross, died, and was resurrected with *all* authority. Let us pray with confidence, knowing that our faces are showing up in hell and demons are fleeing, because greater is He that is in us than he that is in the world. Let it be said of each of us: "They know whose they are and who they are in Christ. They know their authority and they are not afraid to use it." You are seated in heavenly places!

Daily Prayer for Week 7:

Father, I thank you that you have seated me in Christ in heavenly places. I ask that you give me great boldness in proclaiming your Word. Stretch out your hand, oh Lord, with healing power. May I do miraculous signs and wonders through the name of your holy servant Jesus. Fill me with your Holy Spirit. Let me go out and proclaim the Word of God with boldness. (Acts 4:29 – 31)

[1] It Is Well – Kristene DiMarco & Bethel Music – You Make Me Brave. Bethel Music 2014

Daily Meditation for Week 7:

Day 1 Memorize: "And these signs will follow those who believe: In My name they will cast out demons; they will speak with new tongues; they will take up serpents; and if they drink anything deadly, it will by no means hurt them; they will lay hands on the sick, and they will recover." (Mark 16:17 – 19 NKJV)

ACTUALIZE IT: _____

_____

_____

_____

_____

_____

_____

_____

_____

_____

_____

_____

PERSONALIZE IT: _____

_____

_____

Daily Declaration:

I am seated in Christ in Heavenly Places and I have been given power and authority over all strategies of the enemy. I am more than a conqueror through Him who loves me. (Ephesians 2:6, Luke 9:1, Romans 8:38)

Week 7 Day 2 Memorize: "And Jesus came and spoke to them, saying, "All authority has been given to Me in heaven and on earth. Go therefore and make disciples of all nations, baptizing in the name of the Father and of the Son and of the Holy Spirit, teaching them to observe all things that I have commanded you; and lo, I am with you always, even to the end of the age." Amen". (Matthew 28:18 – 20 NKJV)

ACTUALIZE IT: _____

_____

_____

_____

_____

_____

_____

_____

_____

_____

_____

_____

PERSONALIZE IT: _____

_____

_____

Daily Declaration:

I am seated in Christ in Heavenly Places and I have been given power and authority over all strategies of the enemy. I am more than a conqueror through Him who loves me. (Ephesians 2:6, Luke 9:1, Romans 8:38)

Week 7 Day 3 Memorize: "Then He called His twelve disciples together and gave them power and authority over all demons, and to cure diseases. He sent them to preach the kingdom of God and to heal the sick." (Luke 9:1 & 2 NKJV)

ACTUALIZE IT: _____

_____

_____

_____

_____

_____

_____

_____

_____

_____

_____

_____

_____

PERSONALIZE IT: _____

_____

_____

Daily Declaration:

I am seated in Christ in Heavenly Places and I have been given power and authority over all strategies of the enemy. I am more than a conqueror through Him who loves me. (Ephesians 2:6, Luke 9:1, Romans 8:38)

Week 7 Day 4 Memorize: "And He said to them, "I saw Satan fall like lightning from heaven. Behold, I give you the authority to trample on serpents and scorpions, and over all the power of the enemy, and nothing shall by any means hurt you."" (Luke 10:17 – 19 NKJV)

ACTUALIZE IT: _____

_____

_____

_____

_____

_____

_____

_____

_____

_____

_____

PERSONALIZE IT: _____

_____

_____

Daily Declaration:

I am seated in Christ in Heavenly Places and I have been given power and authority over all strategies of the enemy. I am more than a conqueror through Him who loves me. (Ephesians 2:6, Luke 9:1, Romans 8:38)

Week 7 Day 5 Memorize: "And I will give you the keys of the kingdom of heaven, and whatever you bind on earth will be bound in heaven, and whatever you loose on earth will be loosed in heaven." (Matthew 16:19 NKJV)

ACTUALIZE IT: _____

_____

_____

_____

_____

_____

_____

_____

_____

_____

_____

_____

_____

PERSONALIZE IT: _____

_____

_____

Daily Declaration:

I am seated in Christ in Heavenly Places and I have been given power and authority over all strategies of the enemy. I am more than a conqueror through Him who loves me. (Ephesians 2:6, Luke 9:1, Romans 8:38)

WEEK 8 – I AM GOD'S MASTERPIECE
(Ephesians 2:10)

He was the youngest of eight boys. Handsome. Musical. Spirited. Passionate. As a young boy, David was not the obvious choice as warrior. His brothers saw him as their irritating little brother: prideful, insolent, and whose primary responsibility was to care for the sheep. (I Samuel 17:28)

Saul, a mighty warrior himself, instantly dismissed David because of his youth. Saul condescendingly responded to David's indignation by saying, "You are not able to go against this Philistine to fight. You are a child and he is a warrior from his youth." (I Samuel 17:33)

Goliath also underestimated David. Goliath saw David's size, his good looks, his youth, and was offended that his enemy would send such an unworthy opponent to face him. Goliath mocked David's presence, "Am I a dog, that you come after me with sticks?"

David was underestimated. Those around him defined him by his birth order, his good looks, his youth, his job, his past. They could not see the warrior inside of David, the king he was destined to be the man after God's own heart, God's masterpiece created for good works.

Fortunately, David refused to be defined by others, by his job title, by his good looks. David knew the warrior inside of him. David refused to allow other's opinions of him to prevent him from walking in the fulfillment of God's purposes and promises. David knew his age, his handsome looks, his past experiences did not define him, yet could all be used by God. So David refused to take no for an answer. He would not be satisfied until God's purposes were accomplished.

Are you allowing other's descriptions of you to define you? Are others disqualifying you because of your gender, your ethnicity, your denominational or political affiliations, your age, your past? Ignore the voice of your distractors and ask, "God, how do you define me?" I'm sure he will tell you, "You are my beautiful masterpiece, my handiwork, an expression of Me. I fashioned you with purpose, with intention, with the greatest of care. Go and be the you I knitted together in your mother's womb and walk in the purposes I ordained before your conception. Do not allow anyone to say 'no' to the passions I have put inside of you." And then, if you listen carefully, he will reveal what you were called to do. Now, when he speaks that to you, run with it and never allow anyone or anything to disqualify you. You are his workmanship crafted specifically for what He has called you to do!

Daily Prayer for Week 8:

Lord, I thank you for the journey I have begun of knowing who I am in you. I thank you that I am fearfully and wonderfully made. I am your masterpiece created for good works. I am grateful that your love for me does not ebb and flow with my behavior. There is nothing I can do to make you love me more and there is nothing I can do nothing to make me you love me less. I thank you, Father, that you have placed a hedge of protection around me, and I will withstand the wiles of the devil. I ask you Father, give me the right words so that I can boldly explain your mysterious plan, the Good News. Let me speak boldly for you as I should. (Based on Psalm 139:14, Ephesians 2:10, 6:19 & 20)

Daily Meditation for Week 8:

DAY 1 MEMORIZE: "For you created my inmost being; you knit me together in my mother's womb. I praise you because I am fearfully and wonderfully made; your works are wonderful, I know that full well." (Psalm 139:13 – 14)

ACTUALIZE IT: _____

_____

_____

_____

_____

_____

_____

_____

_____

_____

_____

_____

_____

PERSONALIZE IT: _____

_____

_____

Daily Declaration:

I am God's masterpiece, created anew to do good works (Ephesians 2:10)

WEEK 8 DAY 2 MEMORIZE: "For I know the plans I have for you, declares the LORD, plans to prosper you and not to harm you, plans to give you hope and a future. Then you will call on me and come and pray to me, and I will listen to you. You will seek me and find me when you seek me with all your heart." (Jeremiah 29:11-13)

ACTUALIZE IT: _____

_____

_____

_____

_____

_____

_____

_____

_____

_____

_____

_____

_____

_____

_____

_____

PERSONALIZE IT: _____

_____

_____

Daily Declaration:

I am God's masterpiece, created anew to do good works (Ephesians 2:10)

WEEK 8 DAY 3 MEMORIZE: "For we are God's masterpiece. He created us anew in Christ Jesus, so we can do the good things he planned for us long ago." (2:10 NLT)

ACTUALIZE IT: _____

_____

_____

_____

_____

_____

_____

_____

_____

_____

_____

_____

_____

_____

_____

PERSONALIZE IT: _____

_____

_____

Daily Declaration:

I am God's masterpiece, created anew to do good works (Ephesians 2:10)

WEEK 8 DAY 4 MEMORIZE: "For this reason I remind you to fan into flame the gift of God, which is in you through the laying on of my hands. For the Spirit God gave us does not make us timid, but gives us power love and self-discipline." (II Timothy 1:6-7)

ACTUALIZE IT: _____

_____

_____

_____

_____

_____

_____

_____

_____

_____

_____

_____

_____

_____

PERSONALIZE IT: _____

_____

_____

Daily Declaration:

I am God's masterpiece, created anew to do good works (Ephesians 2:10)

WEEK 8 DAY 5 MEMORIZE: "Being confident of this, that he who began a good work in you will carry it on to completion until the day of Christ Jesus." (Philippians 1:6)

ACTUALIZE IT: _____

_____

_____

_____

_____

_____

_____

_____

_____

_____

_____

_____

_____

_____

_____

PERSONALIZE IT: _____

_____

_____

Daily Declaration:

I am God's masterpiece created anew to do the good works (Ephesians 2:10)

WEEK 9 – I AM STRONG IN THE LORD
(Ephesians 6:10)

Goliath was massive – over nine feet tall with armor that weighed over 120 pounds! The skilled warriors of Israel trembled in his presence. Of course, to fight such a formidable opponent, one must don the correct armor. So Saul, David's mentor and also a skilled warrior, dressed David in his armor. It had proven successful for Saul, and so surely it would help keep David safe.

But instead of wearing the armor of experienced warriors, David chose a staff, a few rocks and a sling shot. Most would have predicted his defeat. Who goes into a battle against a giant with such rubbish? Who enters a fight with such non-traditional garb? David and Christians, apparently.

Our weapons of warfare are not like the world's. We do not fight our battles with guns or rifles. We don't protect ourselves with expensive security systems, and we don't change the world through petitions and debates. We understand our battle is not against flesh and blood, it is not against would-be robbers, terrorists, or political viewpoints. Our battle is against darkness, evil, principalities. Our fight is against Satan and all of his angels.

Since our true opponent is not typical, neither are our weapons of warfare. Our weapons are not weapons of might and strength, but they are weapons wielded best when we know our identity in Christ. Our protective armor is given to us by our Father – truth, righteousness, faith, peace, salvation. Our weapons are prayer and the Word of God. With our protective armor securely fastened, we enter battles on our knees, in prayer, declaring the Word of God, knowing our enemy has already been defeated. We enter knowing the battle is rigged, and we are victorious! We enter knowing greater is He that is in us than He that it is in the world.

Friends, the battle rages every minute of every day. Like Goliath, our enemy attempts to intimidate us with lies, accusations, and fear. But we are donned in an unusual armor, like young David. We are armed in truth, righteousness, faith, peace, and salvation. We have prayer and the word as our weapons and we will like David, defeat our enemy. We win!

<u>Daily Prayer for Week 9:</u>

Lord, I thank you that you have made me strong in you and in your mighty power. I daily put on the full armor of God, so that I may stand against the devil's schemes. Thank you for the gift of discernment, that I may recognize that I do not war against flesh and blood, but against power of this dark world and against the spiritual forces of evil in the heavenly realms. With your power within me, I will be able to stand my ground and after everything, I will stand firmly. (Based on Ephesians 6:10-12)

Daily Meditation for Week 9:

DAY 1 MEMORIZE: "Finally, be strong in the Lord and in his mighty power. Put on the full armor of God, so that you can take your stand against the devil's schemes. For our struggle is not against flesh and blood, but against the rulers, against the authorities, against the powers of this dark world and against the spiritual forces of evil in the heavenly realms." (Ephesians 6:10 – 12)

ACTUALIZE IT: _____

_____

_____

_____

_____

_____

_____

_____

_____

_____

_____

_____

PERSONALIZE IT: _____

_____

_____

Daily Declaration:

I wear the armor of the Lord. I am strong in the Lord and in His mighty power. (Ephesians 6:10)

WEEK 9 DAY 2 MEMORIZE: "Therefore put on the full armor of God, so that when the day of evil comes, you may be able to stand your ground, and after you have done everything, to stand. Stand firm then, with the belt of truth buckled around your waist, with the breastplate of righteousness in place, and with your feet fitted with the readiness that comes from the gospel of peace." (Ephesians 6:13 – 15)

ACTUALIZE IT: _____

_____

_____

_____

_____

_____

_____

_____

_____

_____

_____

_____

PERSONALIZE IT: _____

_____

_____

Daily Declaration:

I wear the armor of the Lord. I am strong in the Lord and in His mighty power. (Ephesians 6:10)

WEEK 9 DAY 3 MEMORIZE: "In addition to all this, take up the shield of faith, with which you can extinguish all the flaming arrows of the evil one. Take the helmet of salvation and the sword of the Spirit, which is the word of God." (Ephesians 6:16 – 17)

ACTUALIZE IT: _____

_____

_____

_____

_____

_____

_____

_____

_____

_____

_____

_____

_____

_____

_____

PERSONALIZE IT: _____

_____

_____

Daily Declaration:

I wear the armor of the Lord. I am strong in the Lord and in His mighty power. (Ephesians 6:10)

WEEK 9 DAY 4 MEMORIZE: "And pray in the Spirit on all occasions with all kinds of prayers and requests. With this in mind, be alert and always keep on praying for all the Lord's people." (Ephesians 6:18)

ACTUALIZE IT: _____

_____

_____

_____

_____

_____

_____

_____

_____

_____

_____

_____

_____

_____

_____

PERSONALIZE IT: _____

_____

_____

Daily Declaration:

I wear the armor of the Lord. I am strong in the Lord and in His mighty power. (Ephesians 6:10)

WEEK 9 DAY 5 MEMORIZE: "But thanks be to God, who always leads us in triumph in Christ, and through us spreads and makes evident everywhere the sweet fragrance of the knowledge of Him." (II Corinthians 2:14 AMP)

ACTUALIZE IT: _____

_____

_____

_____

_____

_____

_____

_____

_____

_____

_____

_____

_____

_____

_____

_____

PERSONALIZE IT: _____

_____

_____

Daily Declaration:

I wear the armor of the Lord. I am strong in the Lord and in His mighty power. (Ephesians 6:10)

WEEK 10 – I AM SAVED
(Romans 10:8-9)

When searching for hotel accommodations in a major city, we often search for the perks. Does it include wi-fi, complimentary breakfast, a gym, or free parking? We want as many perks as possible for our money in order to have a pleasant stay at the hotel.

The Father God is not frugal; He is extremely extravagant. However, He is not wasteful, either. In giving His own Son for our eternal salvation, to secure us an eternal place in heaven, He included with Him every perk we would ever need to have a successful stay on this side of heaven.

The word "salvation" is *sotreion* in Greek, and it means welfare, prosperity, deliverance, preservation, salvation, safety. The word "saved" is *sozo* and it means to keep safe and sound, to rescue from danger or destruction, to make well, heal, restore to health, to save from judgment.

Our salvation is a complete package. It was all provided for us when we made Jesus the Lord of our lives. Every benefit was provided for us. Now, there are some in the Body of Christ that would caution us on believing God for healing or prosperity. But let me ask you, if you rented a hotel room for a night that provided free wi-fi, complimentary breakfast, free parking, and a gym, would you hesitate in taking advantage of the perks freely offered? Or would you think, "I paid for these benefits in the cost of my hotel room?" Well, Jesus paid for your health. He paid for your prosperity. He paid for your deliverance. He paid for your safety.

Brothers and sisters, we have been completely and totally saved. In our salvation package, God has provided all that we need to be victorious on this side of heaven. He has given us everything we need to face the difficulties that arise from living in this fallen world. We have been saved – rescued from danger or destruction, made well, and saved from judgment. We have a salvation that prospers, delivers, preserves us.

Friends, enjoy every benefit, every spiritual gift given to us by the sacrifice of Christ. He paid the ultimate price for you. He gave His life.

Because He died, we live for righteousness.
Because He bore our sins, we are immune from the penalty and power of sin.
Because He was wounded, we are healed.
Because He arose, we are redeemed, restored, renewed.
Because He defeated death, we are victorious.
Because He sits, we are empowered.
Because He reigns, we reign.

Enjoy your salvation!

Daily Prayer for Week 10:

Lord, I thank you that I am saved. I confess with my mouth that Jesus is the Son of God and Lord over my life. I believe in my heart that You have raised Him from the dead. Therefore, I am saved. You have given me your Spirit as a guarantee. I am confident that I have an inheritance and I am saved. No one can ever snatch me out of your hands. I am forever yours! (Based on Romans 10:8-9, Ephesians 1:14, and John 10:28)

Daily Meditation for Week 10:

DAY 1 (FORGIVEN) MEMORIZE: "In him we have redemption through his blood, the forgiveness of sins, in accordance with the riches of God's grace." (Ephesians 1:7)

ACTUALIZE IT: _____

_____

_____

_____

_____

_____

_____

_____

_____

_____

_____

_____

_____

PERSONALIZE IT: _____

_____

_____

Daily Declaration:

I am saved – forgiven, healed, prosperous, delivered, safe, rescued, liberated and restored! I can do all things through Christ who strengthens me. I am the righteousness of God. In Him, I am blessed, an heir, seated, accepted and loved. I am God's strong masterpiece!

WEEK 10 DAY 2 (HEALING) MEMORIZE: "When evening came, many who were demon-possessed were brought to him, and he drove out the spirits with a word and healed all the sick. This was to fulfill what was spoken through the prophet Isaiah: "He took up our infirmities and bore our diseases." (Matthew 8:16 & 17)

ACTUALIZE IT: _____

_____

_____

_____

_____

_____

_____

_____

_____

_____

_____

_____

_____

PERSONALIZE IT: _____

_____

_____

Daily Declaration:

I am saved – forgiven, healed, prosperous, delivered, safe, rescued, liberated and restored! I can do all things through Christ who strengthens me. I am the righteousness of God. In Him I am blessed, an heir, seated, accepted and loved. I am God's strong masterpiece!

WEEK 10 DAY 3 (PROSPERITY) MEMORIZE: "Beloved, I pray that you may prosper in all things and be in health, just as your soul prospers." (III John 2 NKJV)

ACTUALIZE IT: _____

_____

_____

_____

_____

_____

_____

_____

_____

_____

_____

_____

_____

PERSONALIZE IT: _____

_____

_____

<u>Daily Declaration</u>:

I am saved – forgiven, healed, prosperous, delivered, safe, rescued, liberated and restored! I can do all things through Christ who strengthens me. I am the righteousness of God. In Him I am blessed, an heir, seated, accepted and loved. I am God's strong masterpiece!

WEEK 10 DAY 4 (DELIVERANCE, SAFETY, & RESCUE) MEMORIZE:

"The Lord is my rock, my fortress and my deliverer; my God is my rock, in whom I take refuge, my shield and the horn of my salvation, my stronghold." (Psalm 18:2)

ACTUALIZE IT: _____

_____

_____

_____

_____

_____

_____

_____

_____

_____

_____

_____

_____

_____

_____

_____

PERSONALIZE IT: _____

_____

_____

Daily Declaration:

I am saved – forgiven, healed, prosperous, delivered, safe, rescued, liberated and restored! I can do all things through Christ who strengthens me. I am the righteousness of God. In Him I am blessed, an heir, seated, accepted and loved. I am God's strong masterpiece!

WEEK 10 DAY 5 (RESTORATION) MEMORIZE: "So I will restore to you the years that the swarming locust has eaten, the crawling locust, the consuming locust, and the chewing locust." (Joel 2:25a NKJV)

ACTUALIZE IT: _____

_____

_____

_____

_____

_____

_____

_____

_____

_____

_____

_____

_____

PERSONALIZE IT: _____

_____

_____

Daily Declaration:

I am saved – forgiven, healed, prosperous, delivered, safe, rescued, liberated and restored! I can do all things through Christ who strengthens me. I am the righteousness of God. In Him I am blessed, an heir, seated, accepted and loved. I am God's strong masterpiece!

Final Words

Dear Friend in Christ,

I pray that this journey through our identity in Christ has strengthened you, encouraged you, but most importantly, helped set you free to be the man or woman that God has called you to be. I encourage you to continue meditating on the scripture. Continue making the scripture a daily part of your lives. Continue to personalize the scripture and see your story in His Story. Continue to see yourself as Christ sees you.

Remember who you are in Christ. You are the righteousness of God. You are a son or daughter blessed with spiritual gifts. You have an inheritance in heaven and on earth. You are seated in Christ in heavenly places. You are accepted, graced with favor, and loved by the Almighty God. You are His beautiful masterpiece, His poem, created for His pleasure. You are a person of strength who can do all things through Christ who gives your strength. You are saved. In essence, my friend, you are mighty in the Lord and a force to be reckoned with. You are ***triumphantly free***! Walk in the confidence of who you are in HIM!

Closing Prayer:

Lord, I thank you for the Word of God I have heard and meditated on over the last 10 weeks. Lord, I declare that this seed that has been sown has fallen on fertile and good ground. Lord, I ask that this word would take root and prosper. Let the word be fruitful in my heart. Lord, I thank you that this word would bear fruit and produce a hundredfold! Lord, I ask that you send your angels to protect this word in my heart. I forbid the enemy from trying to snatch it away. I stand against the enemy, the cares of this world, persecution, tribulation, and the deceitfulness of riches. Nothing, Lord, no spirit in hell or on earth, shall prevent this word from prospering in my heart. I declare today the words spoken over the last 10 weeks will produce fruit and a one hundred fold harvest. (Based on Matthew 13:18 – 23)

Thank you for sharing this Challenge with me.

Triumphantly Free,
Melissa

Melissa G. Bolden

APPENDIX I – Promises for the Righteous

Below are the promises of God for the righteous. You are the Righteousness of God in Christ Jesus. Throughout this study, weekly choose two or three promises for the righteous and meditate, memorize, and make them personal as you quote them.

Surely, LORD, you bless the righteous; you surround them with your favor as with a shield. (Psalm 5:12)

For the Lord is righteous. He loves righteousness; His countenance beholds the upright. (Psalm 11:7)

For God is present in the company of the righteous. (Psalm 14:5b)

The eyes of the LORD are on the righteous, and his ears are attentive to their cry (Psalm 34:15, I Peter 3:12)

The righteous cry out, and the LORD hears them; he delivers them from all their troubles. (Psalm 34:17)

Many are the afflictions of the righteous but the Lord delivers him out of them all. (Psalm 34:19)

I have been young, and now am old; yet I have not seen the righteous forsaken, nor his seed begging bread. (Psalm 37:25)

The righteous will inherit the land and dwell in it forever. The mouths of the righteous utter wisdom and their tongues speak what is just. (Psalm 37:29, 30)

The salvation of the righteous comes from the LORD; he is their stronghold in time of trouble. (Psalm 37:39)

Cast your cares on the LORD and he will sustain you; he will never let the righteous be shaken. (Psalm 55:22)

Then people will say, "Surely the righteous still are rewarded; surely there is a God who judges the earth." (Psalm 58:11)

The righteous will rejoice in the LORD and take refuge in him; all the upright in heart will glory in him! (Psalm 64:10)

But may the righteous be glad and rejoice before God; may they be happy and joyful (Psalm 68:3)

Surely the righteous will praise your name, and the upright will live in your presence. (Psalms 140:13)

The LORD gives sight to the blind, the LORD lifts up those who are bowed down, and the LORD loves the righteous. (Psalm 146:8)

He holds success in store for the upright; he is a shield to those whose walk is blameless. (Proverbs 2:7)

Thus you will walk in the ways of the good and keep to the paths of the righteous. For the upright will live in the land, and the blameless will remain in it. (Proverbs 2:20-21)

The path of the righteous is like the morning sun, shining ever brighter till the full light of day. (Proverbs 4:18)

Ill-gotten treasures have no lasting value, but righteousness delivers from death. The LORD does not let the righteous go hungry, but he thwarts the craving of the wicked. (Proverbs 10:2-3)

The fruit of the righteous is a tree of life (Proverbs 11:30)

The name of the LORD is a fortified tower; the righteous run to it and are safe. (Proverbs 18:10)

Tell the righteous it will be well with them, for they will enjoy the fruit of their deeds. (Isaiah 3:10)

In righteousness you will be established: Tyranny will be far from you; you will have nothing to fear. Terror will be far removed; it will not come near you. (Isaiah 54:14)

Therefore confess your sins to each other and pray for each other so that you may be healed. The prayer of a righteous person is powerful and effective. (James 5:16)

Appendix II - Meditate on God's Blessing for His People

The promises of Deuteronomy are yours because of Christ's obedience. (Deuteronomy 28:1-6)

1. Blessings shall come upon you and overtake you. Blessed shall you be in the city and blessed shall you be in the field. (verses 2 & 3)

2. Blessed shall be your children (natural and spiritual), the crops of your land, your basket and bread bowl. You shall be blessed coming in and going out. (verses 4 – 6)

3. God will defeat your enemies who attack you. They will come at you on one road and run away on seven roads (v 7)

4. God will order blessings on your barns and workplaces; He'll bless everything you put your hands to and the land He is giving you. (v. 8)

5. God will form you as people holy to Him, just as He promised because of the obedience of Christ. (v. 9)

6. You will have favor with people (v. 10)

7. God will lavish you with good things (v. 11)

8. God will throw open the doors of his sky vaults and pour rain on your land on schedule and He will bless the work of your hands. (v. 12)

9. You will lend to many, but you will not need to borrow. (v. 12)

10. You are the head and not the tail. You will always be the top dog, never the bottom. (v. 13)

APPENDIX III - Spiritual Gifts Available To You[2]

Gifts of the Holy Spirit (I Corinthians 12:8-10)

1. Words of wisdom – supernaturally knowing God's will in a situation

2. Word of knowledge – supernaturally knowing information about someone or something.

3. Faith – supernatural ability to believe God about a situation

4. Gifts of Healing – praying for someone and they are supernaturally healed

5. Working of Miracles – a display of power that goes beyond the natural

6. Prophecy – hearing from God and declaring God's purposes and intents over a person's life or a situation.

7. Discerning of Spirits – supernatural ability to detect the realm of the spirits (good and evil) and their activities

8. Different kinds of tongues – supernatural utterance in an unknown language in a public setting.

9. Interpretation of tongues – supernatural ability to interpret tongues given in an unknown language

Gifts of the Father (Roans 12:3 – 8)

1. Prophecy – (see above)

2. Ministry – to love people through general service and meet their spiritual and practical needs

3. Teaching – the supernatural ability to explain the Word and the heart of God

4. Exhortation – To implore, comfort or teach

---

[2] Thomas Nelson New Spirit Filled Life Bible. Executive editor, Jack W. Hayford, Litt.D. pgs 1855 – 1858 Thomas Nelson, 2002

5. Giving – to be generous in your support of the church's needs

6. Leadership – to stand in front and guide people to the purposes of God.

7. Mercy – to empathize with those in need

Gifts of the Son (Ephesians 4:11)

1. Apostles – innovator; one who establishes and extends the work of the Gospel; supervises large sections of the Body of Christ.

2. Prophet – One who is set apart to see ahead and give direction and wisdom to the Body of Christ; calls others into their giftings

3. Evangelist – One who teaches and preaches such that unbelievers come to a saving knowledge of Christ.

4. Pastor – shepherd; nurtures, cares for the spiritual needs of the body of Christ.

5. Teacher – Expounds and study the Word of God and then presents the teaching in a logical, organized, and engaging method to others.

Melissa G. Bolden

78508161R00054

Made in the USA
Columbia, SC
16 October 2017